THE CITY HOME GARDEN

THE CLASSIC USDA FARMERS' BULLETIN NO. 1044
WITH TIPS AND TRADITIONAL METHODS
IN SUSTAINABLE GARDENING AND PERMACULTURE

BY U.S. DEPARTMENT OF AGRICULTURE

ORIGINALLY PUBLISHED IN 1919

LEGACY EDITION
CLASSIC FARMERS BULLETIN LIBRARY
BOOK NO. 1044

Doublebit Press
Eugene, OR

*New content, introduction, and annotations
Copyright © 2020 by Doublebit Press. All rights reserved.*

*Doublebit Press is an imprint of Eagle Nest Press
www.doublebitpress.com | Eugene, OR, USA*

Original content under the public domain. Originally published in 1919 by the U.S. Department of Agriculture.

This title, along with other Doublebit Press books including the Classic Farmers Bulletin Library, are available at a volume discount for youth groups, outdoors clubs, or reading groups.

*Doublebit Press Legacy Edition ISBN
Paperback: 978-1-64389-142-2*

Disclaimer: Because of its age and historic context, this book could contain content on present-day inappropriate methods, activities, outdated medical information, unsafe chemical and mechanical processes, or culturally and racially insensitive content. Doublebit Press, or its employees, authors, and other affiliates, assume no liability for any actions performed by readers or any damages that might be related to information contained in this book. This text has been published for historical study and for personal literary enrichment toward the goal of preserving the American handcraft tradition, timeless trade skills, and traditional artisanal knowledge.

First Doublebit Press Legacy Edition Printing, 2020

Printed in the United States of America when purchased at retail in the USA

INTRODUCTION
Classic Farmers Bulletin Library

The old experts of artisanal trades, country and homestead knowledge, and the woods and mountains taught timeless principles and skills for centuries. Through their timeless books, the old experts offered rich descriptions of how the world works and encouraged learning through personal experiences *by doing*. Over the last 125 years, manufacturing, farming, and construction have substantially changed. Of course, many things have gotten simpler as equipment and technology have improved. In addition, some activities of pre-digital times are now no longer in vogue, or are even outright considered inappropriate or illegal. However, despite many of the positive changes in manufacturing and crafting methods that have occurred over the years, *there are many other skills and much knowledge that have been forgotten.*

By publishing the reprint series of the old USDA *Farmers' Bulletin*, it is our goal at Doublebit Press to do what we can to preserve and share the works from forgotten teachers that form the cornerstone of the history of the American artisans and traditional crafts. So much farm, homestead, and handcraft knowledge was passed to each generation through experience and hard work. An original mission of the US Department of Agriculture was to optimize farm outputs and increase the quality of life on farms through handcrafts, construction, and old-time farm tricks, tips, and skills. In their *Farmers' Bulletin* series, the USDA captured and passed on knowledge that applied to far more than just farmers!

Through remastered reprint editions of timeless classics, perhaps we can regain some of this lost knowledge for future generations. Today's interest in mastery of old handcraft skills, homestead self-sufficiency, and artisanal character has renewed an interest in the old arts. Luckily, the USDA's *Farmers' Bulletin* series contains thousands of pamphlets dedicated to teaching, improving life, and ensuring self-sufficiency to thrive in both the city and on a farm.

This book is an important contribution traditional handcraft and country skills literature and has important historical and collector value toward preserving the American handcraft and outdoors tradition. The knowledge it holds is an invaluable reference for practicing skills and hand craft methods. Its chapters thoroughly discuss some of the essential building blocks of knowledge that are fundamental but may have been forgotten as equipment gets fancier and technology gets smarter. In short, this reprint of the *Farmers' Bulletin* pamphlets was chosen for Legacy Edition printing because much of the basic skills and knowledge it contains has been forgotten or put to the wayside in trade for more modern conveniences and methods.

With technology playing a major role in everyday life, sometimes we need to take a step back in time to find those basic building blocks used for gaining mastery – the things that we have luckily not completely lost and has been recorded in books over the last two centuries. These skills aren't forgotten, they've just been shelved. *It's time to unshelve them once again and reclaim the lost knowledge of self-sufficiency.*

Based on this commitment to preserving our outdoors and handcraft artisanal heritage, we have taken great pride in publishing this book as a complete original work. We hope it is worthy of both study and collection by outdoors folk in the modern era of outdoors and traditional skills life.

Unlike many other photocopy reproductions of classic books that are common on the market, this Legacy Edition does not simply place poor photography of old texts on our pages and use error-prone optical scanning or computer-generated text. We want our work to speak for itself, and reflect the quality demanded by our customers who spend their hard-earned money. With this in mind, each Legacy Edition book that has been chosen for publication is carefully remastered from original print books, *with the Doublebit Legacy Edition printed and laid out in the exact way that it was presented at its original publication.* We provide a beautiful, memorable experience that is as true to the original text as best as possible, but with the aid of modern technology to make as beautiful a reading experience as possible for books that can be over a century old.

Because of its age and because it is presented in its original form, the book may contain misspellings, inking errors from print plates, and other printing blemishes that were common for the age. However, these are exactly the things that we feel give the book its character, which we preserved in this Legacy Edition. During digitization, we ensured that each illustration in the text was clean and sharp with the least amount of loss from being copied and digitized as possible. Full-page plate illustrations are presented as they were found, often including the extra blank page that was often behind a plate. For the covers, we use the original cover design to give the book its original feel. We are sure you'll appreciate the fine touches and attention to detail that your Legacy Edition has to offer.

For traditional handcrafters and classic artisanal enthusiasts who demand the best from their equipment, this Doublebit Press Legacy Edition reprint was made with you in mind. Both important and minor details have equally both been accounted for by our publishing staff, down to the cover, font, layout, and images. It is the goal of Doublebit Legacy Edition series to be worthy of collection in any outdoorsperson's library and that can be passed to future generations.

Every book selected to be in this series offers unique views and instruction on important skills, advice, tips, tidbits, anecdotes, stories, and experiences that will enrich the repertoire of any person who enjoys escaping a bit from today's modern technology-based, cookie-cutter, and highly industrialized skills. Instead, folks seeking to make things with their hands like the old days may find great value from these resurrected instructional manuals from the past. These books were not simply written to be shelved in a library – they contain our history and forgotten methods to make things with real character and energy with a *human* component.

Therefore, to learn the most basic building blocks of a craft leads to mastery of all its aspects. We hope this book helps you along this path with its rich descriptions and illustrations!

About the USDA Farmers' Bulletin Series

Back in the early 1900s, the US Department of Agriculture (USDA) began publication of small pamphlets that were meant to improve the outputs of America's farms, promote self-sufficiency, and help farmers and farming communities thrive. This publication series continued for decades, and volumes were always available when someone wanted to learn more about a specific skill or topic that could come in handy on the homestead.

Each of the 2,000+ volumes specializes in one specific topic, be it growing a certain crop, raising a particular animal, or building a type of farm structure. Each of the pamphlets captured the best knowledge available at that time, which often represented decades or centuries of old farmer knowledge, which we know, is incredibly useful and reliable!

As we continue to blaze paths into the digital frontier, many of these lost "farmers' tips" have become more useful than ever, particularly to folks looking to start homesteads and small-scale farms, as well as those who just want to live more sustainably, simply, and consciously in light of today's factory processed world. The *Farmers' Bulletin* is also highly useful for people who live in cities, as they contain much information for community gardens, urban and rooftop farming, and sustainable living tips.

Unfortunately, many of these print volumes of the *Farmers' Bulletin* are now out of print. Indeed, because these texts are in the public domain, they are easily found and are available on the Internet. However, many of these books that are easily found on the web are often low-resolution photocopies, complete with scribble marks or other distracting spots. For the first time, high-quality, professionally restored *Farmers' Bulletin* reissues are being made by Doublebit Press to increase access to the timeless knowledge that each contains.

This Doublebit Press Legacy Edition republishes this tradition of handcrafted quality and artisanal work. We hope that this deluxe printed edition of this book will help you gain mastery in your craft, as it is presented in the exact form that it was originally published. Even today, the knowledge contained within its pages are timeless and have much to teach!

Finally, as works of art, the USDA *Farmers' Bulletin* issues contain beautiful illustrations and line art that are a sign of simpler, yet authentic times when quality mattered and craftsmanship was king. This collectible volume makes a great addition to the bookshelf of any handcrafter, maker, artisan, farmer, homesteader, or outdoors enthusiast!

Enjoy some old-time, vintage charm when the government actually encouraged you to be self-sufficient with these beautifully illustrated and classic instruction manuals by the USDA!

U.S. DEPARTMENT OF AGRICULTURE
FARMERS' BULLETIN No. 1044

THE CITY HOME GARDEN

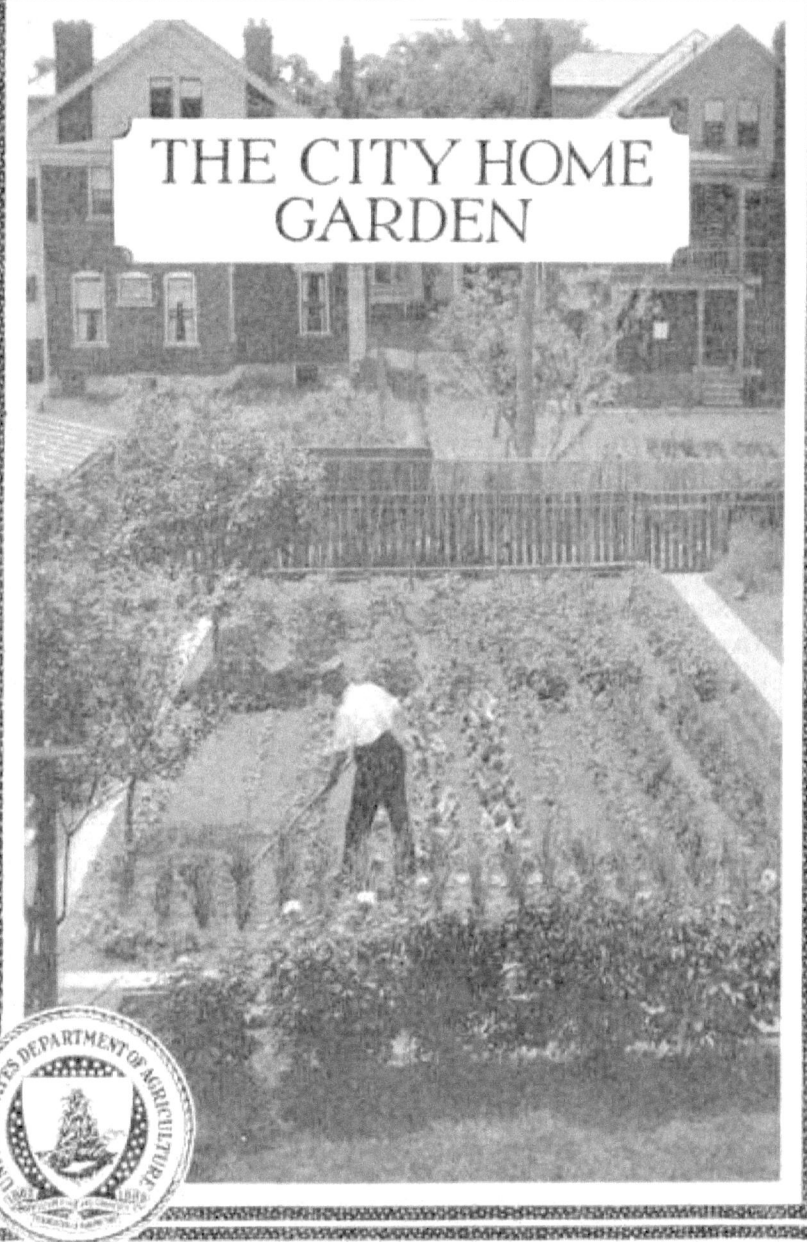

FRESH VEGETABLES for an average family may be grown upon a large back yard or city lot.

The use of fresh vegetables adds variety to the diet and improves the health of the people.

The production of vegetables at home relieves transportation difficulties and solves the marketing problem.

The city home garden utilizes idle land and spare time for food production.

Thousands of acres of idle land that may be used for gardens are still available within the boundaries of our large cities.

Some of the problems that confront the city gardener are more difficult than those connected with the farm garden, and it is the object of this bulletin to discuss these problems from a practical standpoint.

Washington, D. C.   Issued March, 1919; revised June, 1930

THE CITY HOME GARDEN

By W. R. BEATTIE, *Senior Horticulturist, Office of Horticultural Crops and Diseases, Bureau of Plant Industry*

CONTENTS

	Page		Page
Type and location of the city garden	1	Crops for the city home garden	17
Preparation of the soil	3	Beans	18
Use of ashes on garden soils	5	Root crops	19
Liming garden soils	6	Tomatoes	22
Use of manure on garden land	6	Sweet peppers	23
Commercial fertilizers	7	Eggplant	24
Tools	8	Okra, or gumbo	24
Seeds	8	Onions	25
Starting early plants	8	Cabbage group	26
Planting zones	12	Greens and salad plants	27
General care of the garden	16	Vegetables that require considerable space in the garden	29
Holding moisture	16		
Watering	16	Vine group	31
Diseases and insects	17		

THE PROBLEMS that confront the city gardener are vastly greater than those of the farmer, who is free to select the choicest plot of ground upon the farm for his vegetable garden. The city-lot or back-yard garden as a rule offers little choice of soil or location. The available land is often shaded a part of the day, and the soil frequently consists of hard clay or is covered to a depth of several inches with cinders, broken stone, or other materials unfit for growing plants. The city gardener is usually handicapped by lack of practical experience and for want of suitable tools with which to do the work. Hand methods must be employed for the most part, and numerous local difficulties must be overcome. It is possible, however, to grow certain kinds of vegetables under very adverse conditions, and the results obtained by many city gardeners are truly remarkable.

The city back-yard or vacant-lot garden provides a supply of vegetables at home without transportation or handling costs. Vegetables from the home garden are fresher and more palatable than those brought from a distance. Many persons who work in offices, stores, and factories have time mornings and evenings that may well be devoted to the cultivation of a garden, thus utilizing spare time and idle land for food production. The home vegetable garden should be a family interest, and all members of the family who are able to do so should take part in its cultivation. There is no better form of outdoor exercise than moderate working in the home garden, and few lines of recreational work will give greater returns for the time employed. (Fig. 1.)

TYPE AND LOCATION OF THE CITY GARDEN

There are three general types of city vegetable gardens: Back-yard gardens, vacant-lot gardens, and community gardens. In locating the home garden the back yard or the grounds surrounding the dwelling should be given first consideration, because of the convenience both in working the garden and in gathering the products as wanted for use. If the grounds around the dwelling are too small or too densely shaded, or if the soil is of such a character that vegetables can not be grown successfully upon it, the use of a vacant lot in the neighborhood is recommended. (Fig. 2.) Community gardens located in the outskirts of the city, where a tract of land can be secured, are adapted for the use of families living in apartment houses; also for shopworkers and persons employed by large manufacturing concerns. There is a distinct advantage in having the garden located near the home, as much of the work of tending it may be done during spare moments, and the garden can be protected from theft or from injury by stray animals.

Do not locate the garden on land upon which the sun does not shine for at least five hours each bright day. Do not locate the garden on soil where the rock is but a few inches below the surface and where there is insufficient moisture. Do not attempt to grow a garden where a fill has been made with cinders or broken bricks or where the original soil has been buried with materials upon

FIGURE 1.—Small back-yard gardens in a residence section of Washington, D. C.

which weeds will not grow. If weeds grow rank and vigorous it is a sure sign that the soil is good. Do not plant a garden under or near large trees that will steal all the moisture and plant food from the crops. The maples and the oaks are the kinds of trees that are most injurious to crops planted near them. Do not plant a garden on low land where the crops are reasonably sure to be lost from overflow. Failure to observe one or more of these precautions has resulted in disappointment on the part of many gardeners.

Where there is any choice in the selection of a garden location the following points should be considered. The land should be level or gently sloping toward the south or southeast. The drainage should be good, but the land should not be so steep as to wash during rains. The location should be higher than adjoining land, in order to safeguard against frost, as frost does most damage on the lower levels. The ideal soil is a dark sandy loam with a rather retentive subsoil. The soil should be deep and should break up loose and mellow when plowed or spaded. Plenty of organic matter or rotted manure should be present in the soil, in order to give it the power to retain large quantities of moisture and to carry the crops through periods of drought.

The ideal garden spot is seldom found, but it is often possible to choose a location that embodies a number of the more important conditions and then supply others. The difficulties of the first season are greater than those of subsequent years, and a garden plot if properly handled will improve with each season's cultivation.

On account of the wide variety of local conditions that must be met, no definite plan can be given for a garden. A plan should be drawn on paper and the location of each crop decided upon. As a general rule, the rows should run north and south, but it is more

FIGURE 2.—A vacant-lot garden on one of the principal residence streets of Washington, D. C.

important to have the rows run the long way of the garden for convenience in cultivating. Figure 3 shows a well-planned garden.

It is essential that the garden be so arranged that the tall-growing crops will not shade the smaller ones.

PREPARATION OF THE SOIL

With the location of the garden settled, the first step is the preparation of the soil. First, remove anything that would interfere with the plowing or spading of the soil. If the location is the home back yard it is assumed that the ground is free from débris and ready to be broken up. If the garden is to be located on a vacant lot it is probable that there will be stones, broken bricks, tin cans, and other trash to be gotten rid of. If the quantity of trash is not too great it should be hauled to some dump, but if there is so much of it as to make its removal expensive it may be piled on one side or one end of the lot. In some cases stone fences have been built along the outside of lots from the stones that were scattered over the ground.

This cleaning-up process requires considerable work and should be done whenever the weather will permit prior to preparation for planting.

The next step in the garden-making process will be to plow or spade the ground. If the land is in sod it should be turned in the fall so that the sods will rot. Heavy clay soils should be turned up loosely and allowed to lie exposed to the freezing and thawing of

FIGURE 3.—Long straight rows of vegetables which add attractiveness to a garden and lessen the labor of cultivation. Note how this garden has produced these results

the winter months. In all cases manure should be turned under if it can be secured. If the surface soil is so hard that it can not be spaded or plowed to advantage a pick or a mattock should be used and the ground broken to a depth of 8 or 10 inches. Plenty of manure is about the only thing that will bring a soil of this character into condition. The supply of manure in cities is now quite limited, and the city gardener should make arrangements early in the season to get what he needs. It is assumed that the average back-yard garden is about 30 by 60 feet in size. About 1 ton of stable manure can be spaded into the soil of a plot of this size each year. On soil which has not been worked before and which is especially heavy and wanting in organic matter a larger quantity of manure can be used. Street sweepings are not desirable, as they frequently contain considerable oil. Sawdust and planing-mill shavings should not be used on garden land. Leaves may be mixed with heavy soils, but it is best to have them fairly well rotted before they are applied to the land.

Early breaking and exposure to frost is the best method of getting land that has not been under cultivation for a number of years in shape for planting. Sandy soils do not benefit by freezing and thawing as do the heavy clay soils, and in all cases precautions must be taken so that the soil will not wash away during heavy rains. It is a very good plan to plow or spade the land in the autumn, sow rye upon it, and then turn the rye under early in the spring.

In regions where the soil is very sandy it is often necessary to keep the surface covered with coarse manure or with some material to prevent it from blowing away. If this precaution is not taken the entire surface soil will be blown off to the depth of the plowing. In the spring the coarser part of the covering should be raked off before pulverizing and fitting the surface for planting.

Nothing is gained by working the land before it is sufficiently dry in the spring. In sections where the ground freezes hard during winter no harm will be done by plowing it in the fall or during the early winter when quite wet, as the freezing will correct any injury; but land that is worked when too wet in the spring will be injured for the entire season. The usual test is to press a small quantity of the soil in the palm of the hand. If it is too wet for working it will adhere in a solid mass and retain the imprint of the hand, but if dry enough to work it will crumble apart of itself.

When the test shows its fitness for working, land that was plowed or spaded in the fall should be thoroughly harrowed, raked, hoed, or forked over to a depth of 4 or 5 inches, in order to fit it for planting. The more carefully this part of the work is done the easier it will be to care for the crops during the growing season. Land that was not worked in the fall should be plowed or spaded as soon as it dries out sufficiently in the spring, and the top should be thoroughly fitted, as previously suggested.

USE OF ASHES ON GARDEN SOILS

Gardeners frequently ask whether it is advisable to use coal and wood ashes on garden soils. The use of coal ashes on heavy clay soils will tend to lighten them, but the ashes should be screened before they are applied, in order to remove any clinkers or cinders. They should then be spread evenly upon the land and thoroughly mixed with it. Coal ashes have little value as a fertilizer, their use being mainly to loosen the soil and make it more workable.

Wood ashes that are produced by the burning of hardwoods, such as oak and hickory, frequently contain as much as 7 per cent of potash and also a little lime, and for this reason are a valuable fertilizer. Wood ashes produced by the burning of pine and other softwoods, and hardwood ashes that have been exposed to the weather and have had their potash leached from them, have comparatively little value as a fertilizer. Not more than 50 pounds of reasonably dry unleached hardwood ashes should be applied to a plot of ground 30 by 60 feet in size, and these should be well mixed with the soil.

LIMING GARDEN SOILS

Lime improves the texture of certain heavy soils, but its excessive use may prove injurious to most garden crops. As a general rule asparagus, celery, beets, spinach, and sometimes carrots are benefited by the moderate use of lime, especially on soils that are naturally deficient in lime. Most of the garden vegetables do best on soils that are slightly acid, and all vegetables are injured by the application of lime in excess of their requirements. For this reason it should be applied only where it is definitely shown by actual test to be necessary, and in no case should it be applied in large quantities. As a matter of fact most garden soils that are in a high state of fertility do not require the addition of lime. With good drainage, plenty of manure in the soil, and the moderate use of commercial fertilizers, the growth requirements of nearly all vegetables may be fully met.

Where lime is applied it should be spread following plowing and should be well mixed with the topsoil by harrowing. (Fig. 4.) It should not be applied at the same time as, or mixed with, commercial fertilizers or manure, on account of the chemical changes that take place resulting in the loss of nitrogen, and thus destroying the effectiveness of the fertilizers. Lime should not, as a rule, be applied in the fall, on account of its becoming leached from the soil during the winter. Any of the various forms of lime such as hydrated lime and air-slaked lime may be used. In some cases the unburned but finely ground limerock is used, but its action is slower than that of the burned lime. Finely ground oyster shells and marl are frequently used as a substitute for lime. Lime should not be used on land that is being planted to potatoes because of its influence on the development of potato scab.

USE OF MANURE ON GARDEN LAND

The use of barnyard manure on garden land has already been mentioned, but too much stress can not be placed upon this important point. The most successful commercial gardeners not only follow the practice of plowing or spading under large quantities of manure, but they stack up manure to rot and apply the rotted manure as a top-dressing when fitting the land for planting. Beans, tomatoes, and potatoes may be injured by the use of too much manure, but it is practically impossible to have the land too rich for most garden crops.

Poultry and pigeon manures are excellent fertilizers for the garden, but must be used sparingly as they are very strong and are liable to burn the crops. These manures should be kept under shelter until used and then should be well mixed with the soil, care being taken that no lumps of the manure come in direct contact with the seeds. Not more than 200 pounds of poultry or pigeon manure should be applied to a garden plot 30 by 60 feet in size.

Sheep manure is sold by florists and seedsmen and is an excellent fertilizer for garden crops. Like poultry manure, it is very strong and should be used sparingly. A little pulverized sheep manure sprinkled along the rows and worked into the soil will give the plants a vigorous growth.

COMMERCIAL FERTILIZERS

The use of commercial fertilizers is advisable, especially where plenty of stable or barnyard manure can not be procured. As a rule, fertilizers should be sown broadcast and thoroughly harrowed or raked into the upper 3 inches of soil. Where applied underneath the rows the fertilizer should be well mixed with the soil before the seeds are planted. Great care must be taken in the use of commercial fertilizers in a small garden, as there is always a tendency to use too much and thereby do more injury than good. From 40 to 60 pounds of a standard fertilizer, such as is used by truck gardeners, may be applied to a plot of ground 30 to 60 feet in size. A fertilizer containing about 5 per cent nitrogen, 8 per cent phosphoric acid,

FIGURE 4.—Applying lime to a garden after plowing and before harrowing

and 5 per cent potash or one containing about 7 per cent nitrogen, 6 per cent phosphoric acid, and 5 per cent potash is good.

Commercial fertilizers may be used in very moderate quantities as a side dressing for most growing crops. Nitrate of soda is frequently used in this manner, especially with crops that are grown for their leaf and stem development rather than for fruit. Where used as a side dressing it is best to apply the fertilizer a short distance from the plants but where the small feeder roots will reach it. The fertilizer should be worked into the soil immediately.

It should be remembered that the best results are obtained by the use of commercial fertilizers where there is plenty of manure or organic matter in the soil. All sods and weeds and the remains of garden plants that are not infected with disease should be turned under or composted in one corner of the garden, in order to form material with which to enrich the soil.

TOOLS

Elaborate or expensive tools are not necessary for the cultivation of a small garden; in fact, a spade or a spading fork, a hoe, a steel rake, and a line with two stakes to fasten it to are all that are required. A garden trowel and a watering can may be added to advantage but are not absolutely necessary. A wheelbarrow, a wheel cultivator, and a seed drill are desirable for the larger gardens and might be procured and used jointly by several gardeners in a neighborhood. After the soil is broken and in shape for planting, the hoe and the steel rake are the important tools for a small garden.

SEEDS

A comparatively small quantity of seeds is required for planting the average city garden, but these should be procured in ample time and should be of the highest quality obtainable. The best are the cheapest in the long run. Garden seeds should not be wasted; only enough should be planted to insure a perfect stand. Any seeds that are left over should be stored in a ventilated tin or glass container, to protect them from mice until needed for later planting.

The particular variety of any crop to plant will depend upon local conditions. There are usually experienced persons in each community who can be relied upon for advice as to the best varieties to plant in that section. A number of the seed houses offer special garden seed collections adapted to various conditions and sizes of gardens.

STARTING EARLY PLANTS

Half the pleasure and profit of a garden is derived from having something to use just as early in the spring as possible. In many cities and towns each year the local greenhouse men grow thousands of plants which are sold to home gardeners at very reasonable prices. It often happens, however, that home gardeners do not have the opportunity to purchase well-grown plants, so they must start their own supply of early plants in the house or in a hotbed if they desire to have their crop mature early. Among the garden crops that may be started to advantage in this manner are tomatoes, early cabbage, peppers, eggplant, and lettuce. Even cucumbers, melons, squashes, beets, snap beans, Lima beans, and sweet corn may be started indoors by using flowerpots, paper bands, or berry boxes to hold the soil. Early southern-grown plants of cabbage, tomato, pepper, and onion are now being used extensively by northern gardeners.

Where just a few tomato and cabbage plants are desired, the seeds may be sown in a cigar box or in a shallow tin pan with a few holes punched in the bottom for drainage. A very good plan is to secure a soap box and saw off about 3 inches of the bottom portion to form a tray. If the top has been saved it can be nailed on and the box again sawed, forming a second tray. Any shallow box (fig. 5) that may be fitted into the window of a living room where there is a reasonable amount of sunlight will answer for starting early plants.

After filling the trays with sifted soil, smooth off even with the top and slightly firm down the soil in the trays by means of a small piece of board. Use the edge of a ruler or a strip of thin board (fig. 6) to form little grooves or furrows in the soil in which to plant

FIGURE 5.—Window box for starting early plants in the house

FIGURE 6.—Starting early plants; preparing the seed box

the seeds. These little rows should be about 2 inches apart and one-fourth inch deep. Scatter the seeds of tomato, early cabbage, pepper, and eggplant, as shown in Figure 7, very thinly in the rows, and cover them by sifting a small quantity of soil over the entire surface. Smooth the top of the soil gently and water very lightly.

The box should then be placed where the temperature will remain at about 70° F. If conditions are kept right, the seedlings will appear in five to eight days after the seed is planted. From this time on the plants will need constant care, especially as regards watering. Owing to the fact that the light from a window comes from one side only, the seedlings will draw toward the glass, and the box should be turned each day so as to keep the plants from growing crooked. Just as soon as the little plants are large enough to handle they should be transplanted to other boxes and given 2 or 3 inches of space in each direction.

Where the required number of plants is too great for growing in window boxes, a hotbed or a coldframe may be provided. The usual method of constructing a hotbed is first to dig a shallow pit

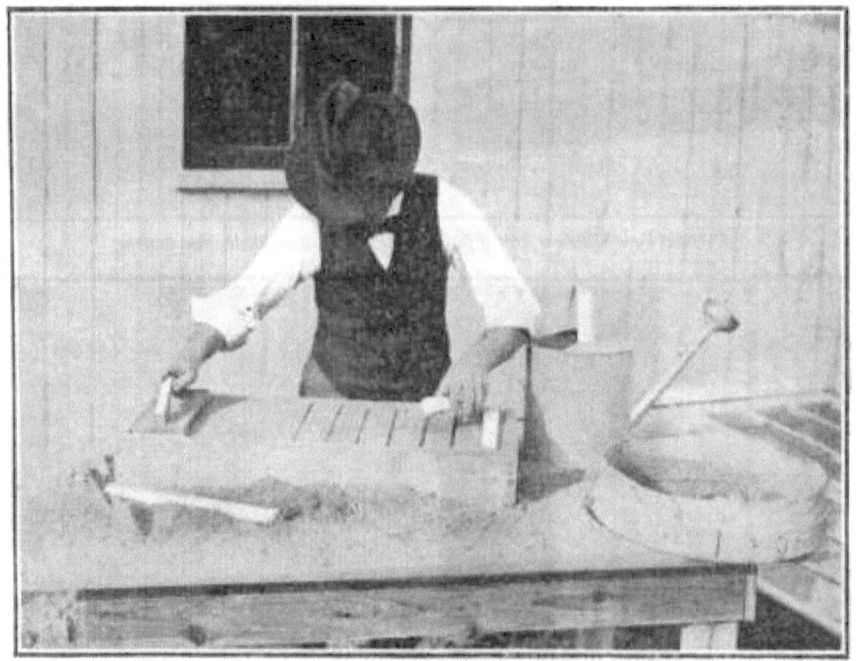

FIGURE 7.—Starting early plants; sowing seed in the window box

8 to 18 inches deep, according to locality, and pack it full of fermenting stable manure. The manure before being placed in the pit should be turned over once or twice in a pile in order to insure even heating. It may then be packed into the hotbed pit and tramped uniformly. Standard hotbed sash are 3 feet in width and 6 feet in length, and the size of the bed should be made to suit the number of sash employed. A framework of boards 18 to 24 inches high at the back and about 12 inches high in front is placed over the manure-filled pit to support the sash. (Fig. 8.)

About 3 or 4 inches of fine garden loam is spread evenly over the manure, and the bed is allowed to stand four or five days to warm up before any seed is sown. At first the temperature of the bed will run rather high, and it is best to delay planting the seeds in it until it begins to decline. This can best be determined by placing a thermometer with the bulb about 3 inches below the surface of the soil and watching it until the temperature falls below 85° F. before planting the seeds.

If glazed sash are not available for covering the hotbed, heavy muslin may be used instead; the glass, however, makes the most desirable form of covering. Care must be taken to give the bed sufficient ventilation to prevent overheating, as it is liable to heat up rapidly when the sun shines full upon the glass. Watering should be done during the early part of the day and the bed given enough air so that the plants will dry off before night. The bed should be closed before evening, in order to conserve enough heat to carry it through the night in good condition. If the weather should turn severely cold, a covering of straw, blankets, or canvas may be thrown over the bed to protect it.

A coldframe is constructed in exactly the same manner as a hotbed, with the exception that no manure is placed beneath it to supply heat.

FIGURE 8.—Preparation of a sash-covered frame for starting early plants

Before the plants are set in the garden, from either the hotbed or the coldframe, they should be gradually hardened to outside conditions by giving them more ventilation each day. Finally, remove the sash entirely on bright days and replace them for the night. The aim should be to produce strong healthy plants that will make a quick start when placed in the garden.

PLANTING ZONES

Tables 1 and 2, together with the frost-zone maps (figs. 9 and 10), are based upon records of the United States Weather Bureau covering a period of 20 years and are intended to serve as a guide for determining the earliest dates that the various garden crops may be planted in the spring, also the latest dates that it will be safe to plant certain crops and have them mature before the first killing frost in the autumn. It should be borne in mind that there is a difference of several days in the frost occurrence within each zone; this is due to differences in altitude and latitude and also to the proximity of bodies of water and large tracts of timber.

Owing to the varied character of the Rocky Mountain and Pacific coast regions, it is not practical to present the planting information in zone form, as there may be a very great difference in the dates of killing frosts in the same general locality, on account of ele-

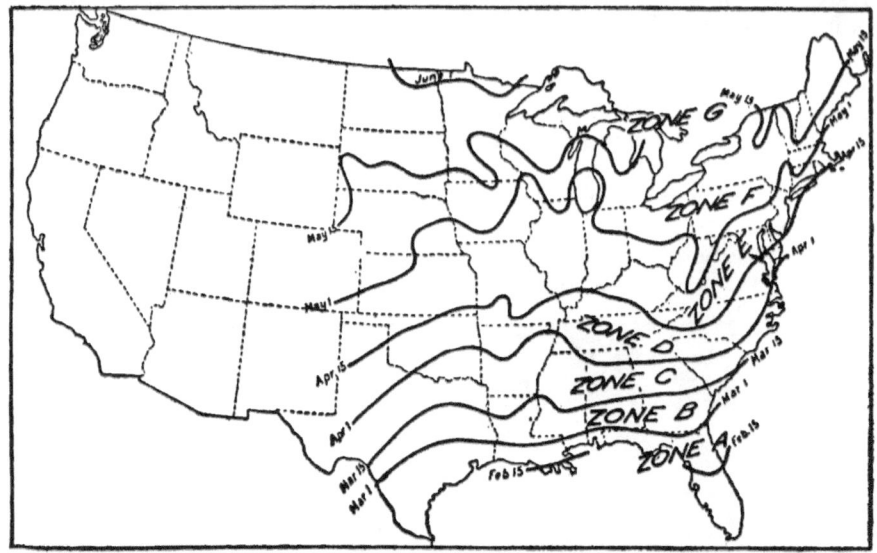

FIGURE 9.—Outline map of the United States, showing zones based on the average date of the last killing frost in spring. The time of planting for the various vegetables is determined for each section by the dates given on this map

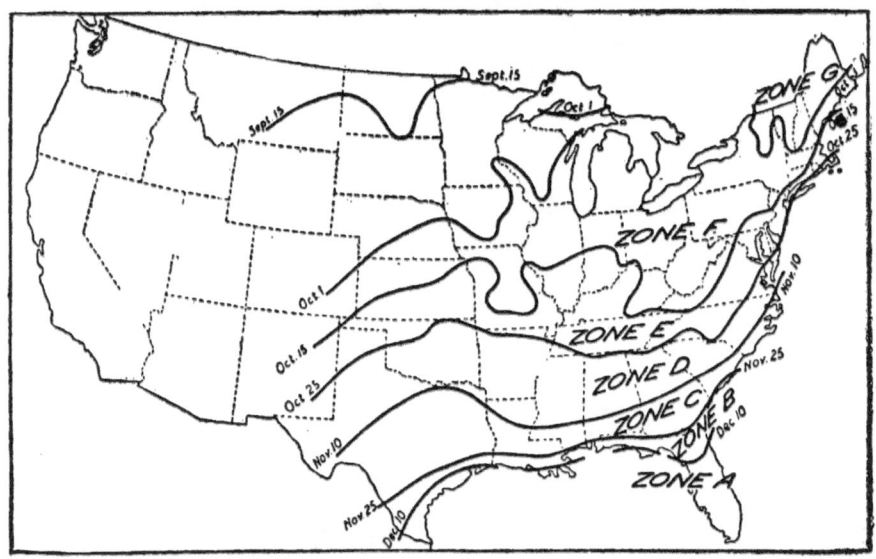

FIGURE 10.—Outline map of the United States, showing zones based on the average date of the first killing frost in the autumn. The latest safe dates for planting vegetables in the autumn are determined by the dates given on this map

vation. Gardeners on the Pacific coast should be guided by the experience of competent persons in their own neighborhood. The coast region of Oregon and Washington is so influenced by ocean currents that a separate map would have to be designed to meet its requirements.

TABLE 1.—*Earliest safe dates for planting vegetables in the open in the zones shown in Figure 9*

Crop	Zone A	Zone B	Zone C	Zone D	Zone E	Zone F	Zone G
Bean:							
Lima	Mar. 1 to 15	Mar. 15 to Apr. 1	Apr. 1 to 15	May 1 to 15	May 15 to June 1	May 15 to June 15	May 15 to June 15.
Snap	Feb. 15 to Mar. 1	Mar. 1 to 15	Mar. 15 to 30	Apr. 1 to May 1	May 1 to 15	May 15 to June 1	May 15 to June 1.
Beet	Feb. 1 to 15	Feb. 15 to Mar. 1	Mar. 1 to 15	Mar. 15 to Apr. 15	Apr. 15 to May 1	May 1 to 15	Do.
Brussels sprouts	do	do	do	do	do	do	do
Cabbage	Jan. 1 to Feb. 1	Jan. 15 to Feb. 15	Feb. 15 to Mar. 1	Mar. 1 to 15	Mar. 15 to Apr. 15	Apr. 15 to May 1	May 1 to 15.
Carrot	Feb. 1 to 15	Feb. 15 to Mar. 1	Mar. 1 to 15	Mar. 15 to Apr. 15	Apr. 15 to May 1	Apr. 15 to May 1	May 1 to June 1.
Cauliflower	do	do	do	do	do	do	Do.
Celery	do	do	do	do	do	do	Do.
Chard, Swiss	do	do	do	do	do	do	Do.
Collard	Jan. 1 to Feb. 1	Feb. 1 to 15	Feb. 15 to Mar. 1	Mar. 1 to 15	Mar. 15 to Apr. 15		
Corn, sweet	Feb. 15 to Mar. 1	Mar. 1 to 15	Mar. 15 to Apr. 1	Apr. 1 to May 1	Apr. 15 to May 15	May 1 to June 1	May 15 to June 15.
Cucumber	Mar. 1 to 15	Mar. 15 to Apr. 1	Apr. 1 to 15	Apr. 15 to May 1	May 1 to June 1	May 15 to June 15	June 1 to 15.
Eggplant	do	do	do	do	do	do	
Kale	Jan. 1 to Feb. 1	Feb. 1 to 15	Feb. 15 to Mar. 1	Mar. 1 to 15	Mar. 15 to Apr. 15	Apr. 15 to May 1	May 1 to 15.
Kohlrabi	Feb. 1 to 15	Feb. 15 to Mar. 1	Mar. 1 to 15	Mar. 15 to Apr. 1	Apr. 1 to May 1	May 1 to 15	May 15 to June 1.
Lettuce:							
Head	do	do	do	Mar. 15 to Apr. 15	do	do	Do.
Leaf	Jan. 1 to Feb. 1	Feb. 1 to 15	Feb. 15 to Mar. 1	Mar. 1 to 15	Mar. 15 to Apr. 15	Apr. 15 to May 1	May 1 to 15.
Melon	Mar. 1 to 15	Mar. 15 to Apr. 1	Apr. 1 to 15	Apr. 15 to May 1	May 1 to June 1	June 1 to 15	
Okra, or gumbo	Feb. 15 to Mar. 1	Mar. 1 to 15	Mar. 15 to 30	Apr. 1 to May 1	May 1 to 15	May 15 to June 1	
Onion sets	Feb. 1 to 15	Feb. 15 to Mar. 1	Feb. 15 to Mar. 1	Mar. 1 to 15	Mar. 15 to Apr. 15	Apr. 15 to May 1	May 1 to 15.
Parsley	Feb. 1 to 15	Feb. 15 to Mar. 1	Mar. 1 to 15	Mar. 15 to Apr. 1	Apr. 1 to May 1	May 1 to 15	May 15 to June 1.
Parsnip	do	do	do	do	do	do	Do.
Pea:							
Smooth	Jan. 1 to Feb. 1	Feb. 1 to 15	Feb. 15 to Mar. 1	Mar. 1 to 15	Mar. 15 to Apr. 15	Apr. 15 to May 1	May 1 to June 1.
Wrinkled	Feb. 1 to 15	Feb. 15 to Mar. 1	Mar. 1 to 15	Mar. 15 to Apr. 1	do	May 1 to 15	May 15 to June 1.
Pepper	Mar. 1 to 15	Mar. 15 to Apr. 1	Apr. 1 to 15	Apr. 1 to May 1	May 1 to June 1	June 1 to 15	May 1 to June 1.
Potato	Jan. 1 to Feb. 1	Feb. 1 to 15	Feb. 15 to Mar. 1	Mar. 1 to 15	Mar. 15 to Apr. 15	Apr. 15 to May 1	
Pumpkin	Mar. 1 to 15	Mar. 15 to Apr. 1	Apr. 1 to 15	Apr. 15 to May 1	May 1 to June 1	June 1 to 15	
Radish	Jan. 1 to Feb. 1	Feb. 1 to 15	Feb. 15 to Mar. 1	Mar. 1 to 15	Mar. 15 to Apr. 15	Apr. 15 to May 1	May 1 to 15.
Salsify	Feb. 1 to 15	Feb. 15 to Mar. 1	Mar. 1 to 15	Mar. 15 to Apr. 1	Apr. 15 to May 1	May 1 to 15	May 15 to June 1.
Spinach	do	do	do	Mar. 1 to 15	Mar. 15 to Apr. 15	Apr. 15 to May 15	Do.
Squash	Mar. 1 to 15	Mar. 15 to Apr. 1	Apr. 1 to 15	Apr. 15 to May 1	May 1 to June 1	June 1 to 15	
Sweetpotato	do	do	do	do	do	do	
Tomato	do	do	do	do	do	May 15 to June 15	June 1 to 15.
Turnip	Jan. 1 to Feb. 1	Feb. 1 to 15	Feb. 15 to Mar. 1	Mar. 1 to 15	Mar. 15 to Apr. 15	Apr. 15 to May 1	May 1 to 15.

TABLE 2.—*Latest safe dates for planting vegetables for the fall garden in the zones[1] shown in Figure 9*

Crop	Zone C	Zone D	Zone E	Zone F	Zone G
Bean:					
Pole Lima	Sept. 15	Aug. 1	July 15	July 1	
Snap	do	Sept. 1	Aug. 15	Aug. 1	July 15
Beet	do	do	do	do	Do.
Cabbage	Sept. 1	Aug. 15	July 15	July 1	June 15
Carrot	do	do	do	do	Do.
Cauliflower	do	do	do	do	Do.
Celery	Oct. 1	Sept. 1	Aug. 1	do	May 15
Chard, Swiss	Sept. 15	do	Aug. 15	Aug. 1	July 15
Corn, sweet	Aug. 15	Aug. 1	July 15	July 1	June 15
Cucumber	do	do	do	do	
Eggplant	July 15	July 1	June 15	June 1	
Kale	Nov. 1	Oct. 1	Sept. 15	Sept. 1	Aug. 15
Lettuce	do	do	Sept. 1	Aug. 15	Aug. 1
Melon:					
Muskmelon	July 1	July 1	June 15		
Watermelon	June 15	June 1	May 15	May 1	
Okra	July 15	July 1	June 15	June 1	
Onion sets	do	do	do	do	May 15
Parsley	Nov. 1	Oct. 1	Sept. 1	Aug. 1	July 1
Parsnip			May 15	May 1	Apr. 15
Pea	Nov. 1	Oct. 1	Sept. 1	Aug. 1	July 15
Pepper	July 15	July 1	June 15	June 1	
Potato	Aug. 15	Aug. 1	July 15	July 1	June 15
Radish	Oct. 15	Oct. 1	Sept. 15	Sept. 1	Aug. 15
Salsify	June 15	June 1	May 15	May 1	Apr. 15
Spinach	Oct. 15	Oct. 1	Sept. 1	Aug. 15	Aug. 1
Squash:					
Bush	Aug. 15	Aug. 1	July 15	July 1	June 15
Vine	July 15	July 1	June 15	June 1	
Sweetpotato	Aug. 15	July 15	do	May 1	
Tomato	do	do	July 1	June 15	
Turnip	Oct. 15	Oct. 1	Sept. 1	Aug. 1	July 15

[1] Zones A and B are sections in which many vegetables are planted late in the fall to form the winter garden or early spring garden.

In zones A, B, C, and parts of zone D of the eastern United States, cabbage, turnip, spinach, kale, collard, and certain varieties of onion may be grown in the open ground throughout the winter. In certain parts of zone E spinach and kale may be grown all winter. In zone F such crops as sweetpotato, melons, eggplant, and peppers should be planted only under the most favorable conditions, as the season is sometimes too short for their full development under adverse conditions.

Garden plants are divided into about four more or less distinct groups.

Early cabbage, kale, onion sets, peas, potatoes, spinach, and radishes may be planted two weeks before the average date of the last killing frost.

Beets, Swiss chard, carrots, lettuce, peas, cauliflower, and sweet corn may be planted about the date of the last killing frost.

Beans, parsnips, salsify, melons, cucumbers, tomatoes, and sweetpotato plants may be planted after the last killing frost.

The heat-loving plants, such as peppers, eggplant, Lima beans, and the squashes, should not be planted in the open until the ground has thoroughly warmed, which will be two to four weeks after the last killing frost.

There are a number of crops, such as snap beans, lettuce, radishes, and beets, that should be planted at intervals in order to insure a continuous supply throughout the season. In the case of snap beans as many as five different plantings may be had in some sections. In the southern part of the United States special attention should be given to the planting of the semihardy crops, such as spinach, kale, and cabbage, during the autumn, in order to have a supply throughout the winter.

By following the planting dates given in Table 2 (see also fig. 10), the various crops will mature during average years; however, there may be seasons when the first killing frost in the autumn occurs earlier than usual and some of the later plantings will be lost. The late planting of vegetables prolongs the season of usefulness and is worth a chance.

GENERAL CARE OF THE GARDEN

A garden bears close acquaintance, and the successful gardener is the one who keeps in close contact with his crops throughout the entire growing season. A visit to the garden during the early morning while the dew hangs heavily upon every plant will reveal the happenings of the night. Perhaps some insect attack has started or some injury has occurred which requires immediate attention. A garden requires a little attention almost every day and responds in direct proportion to the care bestowed upon it. The size of the garden should be such that its care will not prove a burden. A small garden intensively cultivated is much better than a larger one which is allowed to grow to weeds.

HOLDING MOISTURE

The frequent stirring of the surface soil with a steel rake will stimulate the growth of the crops and control weeds. The surface should be stirred after a rain just as soon as the ground is dry enough to work. The stirring of the soil is primarily in order to kill weeds, but there is need of maintaining a loose friable condition and avoiding packing of the soil even where no weeds are present. The roots of plants require air as well as moisture, and frequent stirring of the surface soil admits the air and at the same time conserves moisture. Shallow cultivation during dry weather forms what is known as a soil mulch, preventing the escape of moisture.

WATERING

Artificial watering, if properly applied, will prove a decided advantage during dry periods, but may prove an injury if not properly done. Frequent light sprinkling of the garden is injurious. The proper method is to soak the soil thoroughly about once each week, preferably during the evening, and then loosen the surface by cultivation as soon as the soil is dry enough to work. No more water should be applied until absolutely necessary; then another soaking should be given. On a small scale the water may be applied by means of a sprinkling can. Where available, a garden hose is effective, and overhead sprinkler systems are frequently employed to advantage. Perhaps the best method for applying the water is to open slight furrows alongside the rows of plants and allow the water to flow gently along these furrows.

After the water has all soaked into the soil the wet earth in the furrows should be covered with dry soil to prevent baking. Where seeds are to be sown during a period of drought a slight furrow may be opened and filled with water; then, after the water has soaked into the soil, the seeds may be sown and covered with dry earth. This method will insure a good stand of plants, as the moisture feeds upward in the soil, like the oil in a lamp wick.

DISEASES AND INSECTS

Garden crops are subject to attack by a number of insects and diseases. Preventive measures are best, but if an attack occurs and the city gardener is not familiar with the insect or disease and the proper treatment to protect his crops he is advised to consult the local garden leader or write immediately to the Extension Division of the State College of Agriculture. The United States Department of Agriculture has bulletins containing the necessary information on garden insects and diseases, and these can be procured free upon request.[1]

Small compressed-air sprayers that may be carried by a strap over the shoulder of the operator are very satisfactory for use in the small garden. One of these sprayers will serve for several gardeners in a single neighborhood, and the original cost is reasonable. Wherever poisons are used in the fight against garden insects great care must be taken to see that they are stored in a safe place where there will be no chance of persons or animals becoming poisoned. Garden products such as snap beans should not be sprayed or dusted with poisons after the edible portions form.

Poisons may be applied in powdered form to a number of the garden crops, including potatoes, by means of a small burlap or cheesecloth bag, the poison being dusted upon the plants when they have dew upon them. This can be done in the morning before the plants have dried or late in the evening after the dew has begun to form.

CROPS FOR THE CITY HOME GARDEN

As a rule not more than 10 or 12 different kinds of vegetables should be grown in the city home garden. These should be chosen from the standpoint of securing the greatest food value from a limited area. Certain of the very important food crops, such as potatoes, peas, and sweet corn, require too much space for the small city garden, but should be included wherever the available space will permit.

Owing to the extreme variation of local conditions, no definite plan can be given for the city home garden, and each gardener will have to select the crops to be grown according to his soil, space, and the requirements of his family. By careful planning and by keeping every foot of garden space fully occupied a great quantity of produce can be secured from a comparatively small plot of ground. A succession of plantings of certain vegetables will produce a continuous supply, while others may be grown between the main crops, thus making the land do double duty. There is a tendency on the part of many persons to plant too heavily to lettuce and radishes. As a matter of fact a supply of these vegetables can be grown in the rows between the plants or hills of other crops. Most beginners attempt too many varieties and kinds of vegetables. They would do better

---

[1] For additional information on the insects and diseases of garden vegetables, see Farmers' Bulletin 1371, Diseases and Insects of Garden Vegetables.

to confine themselves to a few standard sorts, leaving the novelties to those who have plenty of land at their disposal.

It is assumed that the average space available for the city vegetable garden will not exceed 30 by 60 feet. Many gardens in back yards are smaller, while others located on vacant lots may include one-fourth acre or more. The size of the garden will determine largely the crops to be grown. The following cultural directions are based on average conditions and are subject to some modification to suit the locality.

BEANS

The bean crop stands at the head of the list in importance for the city garden, especially from the standpoint of producing a large quantity of food quickly on a limited space. The food value of the bean, in all forms, is also very high, and it may be grown under a wide range of conditions.

String beans, or snap beans in bush form, are the most popular for planting in the small garden. The seed should not be planted until the ground is fairly warm and the danger of frost safely passed. Stringless Green-Pod, Bountiful, Currie Rustproof Wax, and Refugee Wax are the leading early varieties of bush beans. Where space is limited the bush varieties can be planted in rows 24 inches apart, with the individual plants 3 or 4 inches apart in the row. Three or even four plantings at intervals of two or three weeks should be made, in order to insure a continuous supply. In sections where the first autumn frost does not occur until about the 1st of October a late or fall crop of snap beans can be grown to advantage, the seed being planted about the first week in August.

A half pint of seed of snap beans will plant about 100 feet of row with four seeds to a hill and the hills 12 inches apart. A hundred feet of row will be sufficient for one planting to supply the average family. If four plantings are made 1 quart of seed will be required.

Pole or climbing beans should be planted in every garden where space will permit. The variety known as Kentucky Wonder produces a plentiful supply that can be eaten pod and all while they are tender, as shelled beans when more mature, and as dry beans after they ripen. Pole or climbing Lima beans are adapted to a wide range of territory and can often be grown on a division fence, on a trellis covering the kitchen porch, or on an outbuilding. Figure 11 shows a street fence which is being made to support a fine crop of Lima beans. Bush Lima beans are less particular in their soil and climatic requirements, but are considered by many persons to be of finer quality than the pole varieties.

Lima beans require a richer soil than string or snap beans, and the seed should not be planted until the ground is quite warm, fully a week later than snap beans. All beans should be planted comparatively shallow, especially on clay or heavy soils. On light or sandy soils beans may be covered from $1\frac{1}{4}$ to 2 inches. Beans will not start well if planted in wet soil or if covered too deeply.

In case the soil should become packed by heavy rains before the plants appear, it is a good plan to break the crust over the row by means of a steel rake, great care being taken that the rake teeth do not go deep enough to injure the sprouting beans. Beans should not be worked when their leaves are wet with dew or rain, as this has a tendency to spread disease.

In case more beans are grown than are required for summer use, the young, tender pods may be canned for winter. Any beans that become too old for immediate use should be allowed to ripen and be saved for planting the next season or for cooking as dry beans. Colored dry beans are as good as white, both in flavor and nutritive value, in spite of a rather general popular belief to the contrary, and none of them should be wasted.

ROOT CROPS

The root crops, including beets, carrots, parsnips, salsify, turnips, and radishes, form a group of very important food crops for the small garden. The soil requirements and general culture are very much the same for all the root crops, and for that reason they are considered collectively. The soil for root crops should be quite

FIGURE 11.—Lima beans growing on the outside of a garden fence

rich, and it should also be spaded or plowed deep and made fine and mellow the full depth that is broken. These root crops will all withstand slight frosts and may be planted very early in the spring. Root crops are especially desirable for the small garden on account of the fact that the rows may be as close together as 12 or 14 inches and the plants 3 or 4 inches apart in the row, making it possible to grow a large quantity of food on a small area.

BEETS

An ounce of beet seed will be sufficient for the ordinary city garden. Beets may be planted almost as soon as the ground can be worked in the spring. Make the soil fine and mellow, then lay off the row about 1 inch deep, using the rounded end of the hoe handle to make the little furrow. What are commonly called beet seeds are really fruits each containing two or three seeds, and for that reason too many should not be put in. Eight or ten to the foot of row are sufficient. Cover the seeds about 1 inch and rake the surface smooth over the row. If the seeds are good and the weather favorable the plants should appear in about 10 days after planting. They should be thinned to about 3 inches in the row, but if not too thick to start with they may be allowed to reach a height of about 3 or 4 inches before thinning, and the thinnings may be used for beet greens. Any skips or spaces can be filled in by transplanting plants that are removed from other parts of the row. A row 50 feet long will furnish enough early beets to supply the ordinary family. A second planting may be made about four weeks after the first. A late planting should be made about six or eight weeks before the first autumn frosts. Any beets that are left in the garden at the end of the season should be stored for winter use.

Crosby's Egyptian and Detroit Dark Red are considered among the best varieties for the home garden.

CARROTS

One-fourth ounce of carrot seed will be more than enough to plant 50 feet of row early in the spring and to make another similar planting later for fall use and storage. Plant the seeds rather thickly, 15 or 20 to the foot, and cover them with about half an inch of light soil, but not more than one-fourth of an inch in heavy soil. Thin to 2 or 2½ inches in the row as soon as they are large enough to handle. If desired, the plants may be left a little closer, then thinned a second time when the first of the young carrots are about half an inch in diameter. The young carrots that are thinned out may be used on the table as creamed baby carrots and are very fine. Late-planted carrots may remain in the ground until after the first frosts of autumn and then dug, topped, and stored in moist sand for winter use.

Oxheart, Chantenay, and Danvers Half-Long are common varieties.

PARSNIPS

A 10-cent packet, or about one-eighth of an ounce, of parsnip seed will be sufficient to plant for the ordinary family. Be sure that the seed is fresh, as it loses its vitality if kept over until the second year. Plant the same as carrots and thin to 3 or 4 inches in the row. Parsnips require a deeply prepared and very rich soil for their best development.

Parsnips may remain in the ground where grown during the winter or until wanted. It may be best, however, to dig part of the roots late in the fall before the ground freezes and store them for winter use.

In the North parsnips are planted quite early and given the entire season to develop and are used mainly during the winter and spring. In the South they may be planted quite early and used as a spring vegetable, and then another planting made for a fall crop. The later planting is usually made in August or September, when the late summer rains occur.

Hollow Crown and Guernsey are among the best varieties.

SALSIFY, OR VEGETABLE OYSTER

Salsify requires practically the same cultural treatment as parsnips. It is not grown extensively in the home gardens of the Southern States, but is primarily a northern crop. Salsify may remain in the ground during the winter, or a part may be dug late in the fall and stored in a bed or box of moist sand for winter use.

The Sandwich Island is the leading variety.

TURNIPS

Throughout the Northern States turnips are planted as a late-season crop, the seed being sown from July 10 to August 1 and the crop harvested after the first heavy frosts. In the Southern States turnips are planted in the spring, just as soon as the ground can be worked, and the crop is used before the hot weather of summer comes on. A late crop is frequently planted in September, the roots being cooked in the usual manner, while the young tender tops are boiled as greens.

For the small garden, turnips had best be planted in drills, with the rows about 12 inches apart, and the plants should be thinned to 2 or 2½ inches in the row. The seed should be scattered very thinly in the drill and covered very lightly. The plants removed in thinning may be used as greens. Turnips will withstand some frost, but their keeping qualities are injured if they are allowed to freeze before pulling. If they become frozen in the storage pit they should not be disturbed until the weather warms and they gradually thaw out. For best results turnips should not actually freeze at any time.

The Purple-Top Strap-Leaved is a leading variety.

RADISHES

Everybody wants a few early radishes in the garden, because they come to maturity quickly and furnish something green and succulent for the table. From 10 to 20 feet of row will produce all the radishes required by a family. The seeds should be sown in a little furrow or drill, about 12 or 15 seeds to the foot, and covered 1 inch. Radishes may also be sown thinly in the drill with beets, carrots, or parsnips, as they come quickly and break the surface for the other seedlings. The radishes should be pulled before they are large enough to injure the crop with which they are sown.

Scarlet Globe White-Tipped, French Breakfast, Icicle, and Long Scarlet Short Top are among the leading varieties.

Where it is desirable to have radishes for a considerable period of time, two or even three plantings at intervals of two weeks should be made, or the same result may be attained by the proper selection of varieties. There are also varieties of winter radishes that may be planted late in the summer for winter use. Long Black Spanish and China Rose are large, firm, pungent sorts.

TOMATOES

Tomatoes are among the most universally used products of our home gardens, and there should be a few plants, no matter how small the garden. In order to have tomatoes early, the seeds must be sown in the house or hotbed or the plants purchased from some plant grower who has the facilities for starting them early. Bonny Best,

Earliana, Acme, and Early Detroit are among the leading early sorts, while Marglobe and Stone are standard intermediate and late varieties. Two small packets of seed, one of an early and one of a late variety, will produce enough plants for several family gardens, and it may be possible for one person to start the plants for an entire neighborhood. If a window box is used for starting early plants of various kinds, a portion of the space in this box should be used for the tomato plants. Where a window box is not in use a cigar box filled with loose soil will serve as a seed bed, but the plants will have to be transplanted and given about 3 inches of space both ways as soon as they form one or two true leaves in addition to their two small seed leaves. Tomato seed comes up in about 8 to 10 days, and the seedlings will ordinarily be ready for transplanting in 2 weeks after the seed is sown. About 6 to 8 weeks will be required for growing the plants from the time of sowing the seed until they are ready for setting in the garden.

A tray of fine, rich soil about 3 inches deep placed in a south window of a living room makes a good transplanting bed. The plants can be grown in quart berry boxes, in 3-inch flowerpots, or in paper bands. The essentials are to keep the plants growing rapidly from the start and to retain all the dirt attached to their roots when setting them in the garden.

The best method of growing tomatoes in the small home garden is by pruning the plants to a single stem, or at most to two stems, and tying them to stakes or a trellis, as shown in Figure 12. By this method the plants can be set as close as 2 feet apart in each direction. When tied to stakes the plants are easy to cultivate. The fruit is clean because it is kept off the ground, and the tomatoes ripen earlier than when the plants are not pruned or tied to stakes. Any stakes that are about 1½ inches in diameter and 4 to 5 feet long will answer. Frequently the plants are trained to horizontal wires stretched on small posts or to a trellis made of laths.

The tomato plants are pruned by pinching out the side shoots (fig. 12) as they appear in the axil of the leaf; that is, where it joins the main stem. The fruit clusters appear on the opposite side of the stem where there is no leaf. The plants are tied to the stakes or other support by means of soft twine or with small strips of old cotton goods. (Fig. 13.) Jute string is especially suitable for tying tomatoes. Loop the string around the stake so that it will not slip downward on the stake, and then tie loosely below a leaf node in such a manner that the stem will be supported without the string binding it and injuring its growth.

Four to seven fruit clusters will be formed on each plant, and if the plants are well cultivated and cared for they will continue to bear fruit throughout the season in the northern parts of the country. In the South, where the heat of midsummer kills tomato plants, a late crop may be planted for fall use.

SWEET PEPPERS

Sweet peppers are increasing in favor with home gardeners everywhere. Six or eight good plants will supply enough for an ordinary family. In the North, where the growing season is short, the plants must be started indoors and should be transplanted twice, so as to be quite large by the time the weather is warm enough to set them in the garden. Pepper plants will not withstand any frost, and they should not be set out until all danger is past. In the South the seed should be sown in the house or in a hotbed, and the young plants may be transplanted directly from the seed bed to the garden, although better plants will be obtained if they are transplanted first from the seed bed to other boxes or to the hotbed and later to the garden. The plants should be handled in the same manner as tomatoes, but pepper plants are even more delicate.

The Ruby King, California Wonder, World Beater, and Chinese Giant are standard varieties of the large sweet peppers. Pimento

FIGURE 12.—Training tomatoes to stakes: A, Cutting out the side shoots or branches; B, tying the main stem to the supporting stake

peppers are becoming very popular throughout the Southern States; however, they will not mature where the frost-free growing season is less than four and one-half months, and they are not profitable unless they have at least five months of warm weather for their development. The pimento is adapted to the South, where the summers are long, with plenty of hot weather. The green pimento peppers have a thick flesh and a pleasant flavor and may be used like any sweet pepper. When red ripe the pimentos are canned for winter salads and for mixing with cheese to make pimento cheese.

EGGPLANT

The seeds of eggplant should be sown indoors at the same time that early tomatoes and peppers are planted. The small plants should be transplanted to pots or paper bands and kept in the house until the weather is quite warm. The plants require a rich, deep soil, with plenty of fertilizer. They should be set about 3 feet apart each way. Five or six plants will be sufficient to supply the average family.

OKRA, OR GUMBO

Okra is sown in the open after danger of frost is over and the soil has become quite warm, but in the North a few plants for the home garden may be started indoors, like tomatoes or peppers. Sow the seed a few inches apart in the row and thin the plants to 18 inches to

FIGURE 13.—Tomatoes trained to stakes in a back-yard garden

2 feet apart. Okra is very prolific, and 8 to 10 feet of row will supply the needs of an average family. Give frequent shallow cultivation until the plants are nearly grown.

The pods are the part of the plant used for food and should be gathered while still crisp and tender. If the pods are removed so as to allow none to ripen, the plants will continue to bear until killed by frost.

The White Velvet, Dwarf Green Prolific, Perkins Mammoth, Long-Podded, and Lady Finger varieties are recommended.

ONIONS

The usual method of growing onions in the home garden is to plant a quart or two of sets just as early in the spring as the ground can be worked. Throughout the South the sets may be planted in the autumn and the surface of the ground mulched with fine straw or light manure over the winter. Onions may also be grown from seed, sown in the early autumn in the South and in the early spring in the North, but as a rule it is more satisfactory to secure a few sets for planting.

Onions require a light, mellow, rich soil. If planted in rows the sets (fig. 14) should be placed by hand, root end downward, about 3 inches apart in the row and covered to a depth of 1 inch. If planted in a bed they should be spaced 4 to 6 inches apart in each direction. As a rule, onion sets are not sold under variety names, but are classed as white, brown, red, or yellow.

FIGURE 14.—Planting onion sets; every bulb is placed with the root end downward at a uniform depth and in straight rows

Southern-grown onion plants are frequently employed for planting in home gardens. These plants are a little less expensive than sets and usually produce a better grade of mature or keeping onion. They should be planted in rows 12 to 18 inches apart, with the plants 3 to 4 inches apart in the rows.

The Yellow Globe, Yellow Danvers, Red Wethersfield, and Silverskin are among the leading varieties that are planted from seed. The Crystal Wax and Red Bermuda varieties of the Bermuda type are often grown in the Southern States.

Where wanted for green onions, the sets may be planted as a filler in the rows with other early crops, but where mature onions are desired it is best to plant them alone. Fully grown onions should not be pulled until the tops have broken over and partially ripened.

The bulbs should then be pulled and spread in a cool, dry place where they will get plenty of air. The mature onions should be kept where it is quite cool and dry.

CABBAGE GROUP

The cabbage group includes both the early and the late types of cabbage, cauliflower, broccoli, kale, collards, Brussels sprouts, and kohlrabi. The general cultivation of each member of this group is practically the same, and they may be grown in almost any locality; in fact, cabbage is one of the most universally grown of our garden crops. The important consideration is to have plenty of plant food in the soil so that they will make a quick, tender growth.

EARLY CABBAGE

Only a few heads of early cabbage should be grown in a small city garden. The plants should be started indoors, but may be set in the garden quite early if hardened off a little before setting them. In certain sections of the South the early varieties of cabbage may be planted in the fall and matured the following spring. The Jersey Wakefield, Charleston Wakefield, Golden Acre, Glory of Enkhuisen, and Copenhagen Market are the leading early varieties. They may be set in rows 24 to 30 inches apart and 15 inches apart in the row.

LATE CABBAGE

Late cabbage can be planted between the rows of early potatoes or after early snap beans, so that double service may be obtained from the soil. All Seasons and Danish Baldhead are among the best late varieties. They should be planted in rows 30 inches apart and 18 inches apart in the row. Cabbage may be stored in a cool, dry, well-ventilated cellar or buried in an outdoor pit in the garden.

CAULIFLOWER

Cauliflower is much more difficult to grow than cabbage and is only adapted to certain soil and climatic conditions which are to be found near the seacoast and in limited inland areas. The important consideration in growing a spring crop of cauliflower is to have it so early that the heads will be formed before the extremely hot weather begins. The methods of starting the plants and general culture are the same as for early cabbage. When the heads begin to form, the leaves should be brought together above the heads and fastened by means of a string, so as to shut out the sunlight and retain the snowy whiteness of the heads. A fall crop of cauliflower can be grown in the same manner as late cabbage. Cauliflower can not be stored to advantage, but should be used within a few days after it is gathered.

KALE

Kale can be grown either as a spring or a fall crop, and in sections where the temperature does not go below zero during the winter it can be planted in the fall and will be ready for use during March and April. The market gardeners around Norfolk, Va., grow great fields of winter kale, planting the seed in September and cutting the crop at any time during the winter when the ground is free from snow and ice. About 50 or 60 feet of row in the home garden may be planted during the late summer for fall and winter use. Kale is not stored, but is left growing until wanted for use.

COLLARDS

No southern garden would be quite complete without a small plot of collards for late fall and early winter use. Collards are a hardy form of cabbage which produce a cluster of very tender leaves that are used in much the same manner as cabbage. Throughout the South collards are planted during the latter part of the summer and the plants are left standing where grown, like late cabbage, and are quite hardy; in fact, it is claimed that the flavor is greatly improved by a slight freezing. Collards are not recommended for planting in the Northern States. A small packet of seeds is all that is necessary to start the plants required in a family garden.

BRUSSELS SPROUTS

Brussels sprouts are a kind of cabbage that forms a large number of buttons or small heads along its stem where the leaves are attached. The culture of Brussels sprouts is the same as that of cabbage except that the leaves are removed from the lower part of the stem to give the buttons more room to develop.

KOHLRABI

Kohlrabi is a near relative of cabbage. It forms an enlargement of the stem just above the surface of the ground. This portion is used in the same way as turnips.

GREENS AND SALAD PLANTS

As a general rule, the American people do not eat enough green vegetables, commonly referred to as salads. Crops of this class are especially adapted to the small garden, as they occupy very little space and will withstand more or less shading. The salad plants require a deep, rich soil, with plenty of moisture. They also thrive under comparatively cool conditions.

SWISS CHARD

Swiss chard resembles the common garden beet in appearance, but it does not form an edible root, like the beet, and is grown for its large leaves, which are boiled for greens. Beet tops while young and tender make good greens, but the leaves of Swiss chard have a very excellent flavor and remain tender a long time. As the outer leaves are removed the plants keep on forming new leaves in the center, so that a continuous supply is provided.

Swiss chard is planted and cultivated the same as garden beets. One-half ounce of seed will be sufficient for the ordinary family of five persons. The variety known as Lucullus is considered best. Plant in the early spring the same as beets, and thin the plants to about 6 inches in the row.

SPINACH

Spinach thrives in cool weather and should be grown both as a spring and as a fall crop. In the extreme northern part of the country only one crop may be grown. In sections where the winters are mild the seed can be planted in the fall and the plants can remain in the ground all winter. For a spring crop, plant in the open ground as soon as the soil can be worked. The rows may be as close as 7 inches, and 12 to 15 seeds should be sown to a foot of row, the plants being thinned so that they will have 1½ to 2 inches of space for their development.

Spinach requires a very rich soil in order to make it grow quickly. A bed 5 feet wide and 30 feet in length and having about eight rows running the length of the bed will furnish enough spinach for the ordinary family. The entire spinach plant is removed by cutting just above the surface of the ground. Four ounces of seed is sufficient for a bed of 5 to 30 feet in size. Spinach is especially desirable as a part of the diet in the early spring.

CELERY

There is nothing particularly difficult about growing celery after the plants are started. The celery seed bed requires very careful watering until the plants are up and large enough to transplant. As a rule, it will be best for city gardeners to purchase plants that are ready for setting in the garden. Celery requires a rich soil and plenty of moisture.

Golden Plume and Easy Bleaching are among the best varieties for the home garden.

LETTUCE

No early garden would be complete without a bed of lettuce; however, only a small space is necessary to grow plenty for the average family. In the old-fashioned garden a small bed was spaded in one corner and the seed sown broadcast and raked into the soil just as soon as the ground was dry enough to work in the spring. As the plants grew and began to crowd one another they were thinned, and those that were pulled out were used on the table. Later, when the plants became larger, they were cut off just above the ground.

Lettuce requires very rich soil and plenty of moisture, will not withstand continued hot weather, and is one of the few crops that can be planted in back-yard gardens that are shaded a portion of the time. A 5-cent packet of seed will produce all the plants required for the small garden. A good method is to sow the seed in a box in the house and transplant the small plants to a bed or to rows in the garden. Lettuce is not injured by a light frost, especially if the plants have been grown in the open. The seed or plants may be planted between other crops that require a longer period for their development than lettuce. Two plantings should be made in the spring and one in the late summer, in order to have a supply for a considerable period.

Grand Rapids and Early Curled Simpson are the leading varieties of loose-leaf lettuce, while Big Boston, Iceberg, New York, Hansen, May King, and California Cream Butter are good heading sorts.

VEGETABLES THAT REQUIRE CONSIDERABLE SPACE IN THE GARDEN

There are a number of garden vegetables that require too much space for growing in the very small home garden. Among those included in this group are potatoes, sweetpotatoes, peas, sweet corn, squashes, muskmelons, and watermelons.

POTATOES

Potatoes are among the first crops that can be planted in the spring. They have no place in a small garden, but where space is available they should be included. A peck of seed potatoes, properly cut, will plant 300 feet of row and should yield 4 to 5 bushels. The usual method is to cut the seed two eyes to each piece, dividing the fleshy part of the potatoes as equally as possible. The seed should not be cut until the ground is all ready to receive it. Great care should be taken to get seed that is free from scab or other diseases.

Potatoes can be planted in the North just as soon as the frost is all out of the ground and the soil dry enough to work. In the South the planting date will be governed by the season and the time that the young plants will be safe from spring freezes. It generally takes three to five weeks after planting in the Southern States for the potatoes to come up. In the North they will appear in a shorter period if weather conditions are favorable.

PEAS

Peas, often called English peas, require considerable space. In order to be of real value, at least 15 feet of row should be planted for each person in the family. Peas are one of the first crops that can be planted in the spring. In the North this planting can be made just as soon as the ground can be worked, and two or even three plantings should be made in order to have a continuous supply. The later plantings rarely yield as well as the earlier ones. In the South peas are planted about the same time as early potatoes, or a little earlier.

Peas require a rather rich soil with a little fertilizer added, as they make a quick growth. First spade and rake the ground until it is fine and mellow, then open a furrow 2 to 3 inches deep with the corner of a hoe. Scatter the seeds broadcast in the furrow, or space them at the rate of 12 to 15 peas to a foot, and cover them. In heavy soils the seeds should not be covered so deeply as in light or sandy soils. If the ground is cold, the seeds may be 10 days or 2 weeks in coming up, and if there should be a heavy rain meantime the crust forming on the surface of the soil should be carefully broken over the rows with a steel rake.

Little Marvel, Alaska, Gradus, and Thomas Laxton are among the leading early sorts. The Champion of England and Telephone are considered good medium and late varieties.

The extra-early sorts may be planted with the rows as close as 24 inches apart where hand cultivation is practiced. The later and larger growing varieties require a space of about 3 feet between the rows. For securing the best yields the late maturing as well as the early maturing sorts should be planted early.

Several of the early varieties of peas can be grown without supports, but they do better if given something to climb on. The late varieties for the most part make a strong growth and require supports. Brush, where it may be had, woven-wire netting, a wire fence, or strings on stakes make satisfactory supports for peas. The supports should be in place when the peas come up, in order that the plants may climb them from the first. Early spring peas occupy the land a comparatively short time and may be followed by late cabbage, beets, turnips, kale, spinach, or some other crop. A planting of peas made late in the summer will often give a fall crop that is ready for use just before frost in the autumn.

SWEET CORN

Sweet corn requires so much space that it should be grown only in large gardens. The rows should be at least 3 feet apart and the individual plants 15 to 18 inches apart if in drills, and 2½ feet apart if in hills of three plants each for early varieties and 3 feet for late large sorts. Corn requires a rich soil and should not be planted until the ground has warmed considerably. A pint of seed will plant 400 to 500 feet of row in either drills or hills. Cover the seed 1½ to 2 inches deep and thin to three stalks in a hill or to single stalks 15 to 18 inches apart in drills.

Golden Bantam, Early Evergreen, and Howling Mob are leading early varieties. Country Gentleman and Stowell Evergreen are among the leading medium and late varieties. For a continuous supply, plant Golden Bantam as early as possible, then follow in a few days with Howling Mob. Two weeks later plant Country Gentleman or Stowell Evergreen and follow with additional plantings of some good late variety every three weeks until midsummer.

SWEETPOTATOES

For an early crop, sweetpotato plants are started in a hotbed, and they must not be set in the open until all danger of frost is past and the ground is well warmed up. They usually thrive best when planted on wide ridges some 3 to 4 feet apart and 12 to 15 inches apart in the row. Any good garden fertilizer will answer for this crop, and it is best applied either in small trenches or to the surface of the ground before the ridges are thrown up. Frequent shallow cultivation should be given until the vines begin to run.

The Porto Rico and Nancy Hall are recommended for moist-fleshed sorts and the Big-Stem Jersey, Goldskin, and Yellow Jersey where dry-fleshed sweetpotatoes are desired.

VINE GROUP

The vine group includes cucumbers, summer and winter squashes, muskmelons, and watermelons.

Practically all of the vine crops can be trained to a wire fence or trellis or on wire netting. By this method they can be planted along a fence or beside a building where there is good sunlight, and the vines can be trained up out of the way of other crops. In case cantaloupes or squashes are grown on a trellis, it will be necessary to support the fruits by means of bagging or cloth slings.

All of the vine crops require plenty of fertility in the soil. In addition to a shovelful of manure and a handful of fertilizer in each hill, a small quantity of commercial fertilizer may be worked into the soil around each hill after the vines begin to spread over the ground. The fertilizer should not be placed closer than a foot from the base of the plants and should be scattered over a considerable area. The space required by these crops precludes them from the small garden except where they are trained on wire or on a trellis, as already indicated. Beginners are advised to grow only summer squash and cucumber, if any.

CUCUMBERS

One or two hills will produce enough cucumbers for the average family. Each hill should be given about 50 square feet of space, or 7 feet in each direction. The hills should be made several days before planting, with a shovelful of manure mixed thoroughly with the soil of each hill. About a dozen seeds should be scattered in each hill and covered to a depth of about an inch. Later, the plants should be thinned to two or three in a hill.

Cucumbers are very susceptible to cold and should not be planted until all danger of frost is past. The plants may be started indoors by planting the seeds in pots, paper bands, or quart berry boxes filled with soil; then set in the garden when the weather is warm. The young cucumber plants are frequently destroyed by a small beetle. The easiest way to protect the plants is by covering the hills with fine wire netting.

Arlington White Spine is a common variety.

MUSKMELONS

Muskmelons, usually called cantaloupes, are grown in exactly the same way as cucumbers. The Netted Gem, Emerald Gem, Eden Gem, Burrell Gem, Early Hackensack, Hearts of Gold, Tiptop, Hoodoo, and Hale Best are among the leading varieties.

WATERMELONS

Watermelons require too much space for planting in a small garden. The cultivation of watermelons is practically the same as that of squashes. The Kleckley Sweets and Florida Favorite are among the best small watermelons for home growing.

SQUASHES

Two varieties of summer squashes are suited for growing in city gardens. These are the Summer Crookneck and Pattypan. The summer squashes are of bush habit of growth and do not require much space. Three to five hills of either of the kinds mentioned will supply the ordinary family. The hills should be 4 to 5 feet apart. Plant 8 or 10 seeds to a hill, covering them to a depth of an inch, and when the plants are well established thin them to three in a hill.

The Hubbard squash and Boston Marrow form true vines and require more space than the summer bush varieties. The fruits of the summer varieties are used while they are young and tender, but those of the fall and winter varieties are allowed to get fully ripe before being gathered and stored. Four or five hills will be sufficient, and a space of 10 to 12 feet should be allowed between the hills.

www.ingramcontent.com/pod-product-compliance
Lightning Source LLC
Chambersburg PA
CBHW021134080526
44587CB00012B/1291